CW01431513

Original title:
The Inner Light

Author: Paula Raudsepp
ISBN HARDBACK: 978-1-80561-008-3
ISBN PAPERBACK: 978-1-80561-569-9

Memories of Light

In dawn's embrace, soft whispers rise,
Echoes of laughter, beneath vast skies.
Flickering moments, gentle and bright,
Held in the heart, like stars in the night.

Time may wash over, like waves on stone,
Yet, boundless memories still feel like home.
In every shimmer, in every spark,
Lives the warmth that ignites the dark.

Glowing Truths

Amidst the chaos, a flame burns true,
Illuminating paths, guiding us through.
In shadows we wander, yet never lose sight,
Of the glowing truths that shine in the night.

Each flicker a lesson, each spark a sign,
In the labyrinth of life, we seek to align.
Through valleys of doubt, where we often stray,
The glow of our truths leads us back to the way.

A Dance of Shadows

Beneath the moon's gaze, shadows entwine,
Whispering secrets, ancient and divine.
A ballet of silence, in the dark they sway,
Embracing the night in a mystical play.

With each step they take, a story unfolds,
Of dreams and desires, of heartaches retold.
In twilight's embrace, they weave and they spin,
Drawing us closer, inviting within.

Inner Radiance

From deep within, a light starts to grow,
Flames of courage, vibrant and slow.
In shadows we falter, yet brightly we shine,
Connecting to all, a unity divine.

Through storms of emotion, we harness our fire,
Burning with passion, igniting desire.
With each breath we take, let our spirits ignite,
For within every heart lies infinite light.

Twilight's Embrace

In the hush of fading light,
Soft whispers dance through night.
Stars blink open one by one,
As day retreats, the shadows run.

Cool breezes stir the leaves so sweet,
Nature's melody, a gentle treat.
Colors blend in muted grace,
Wrapped within twilight's embrace.

A canvas painted in deep hues,
The sky adorned with darkened blues.
Night unveils her secret art,
In the quiet, we find our heart.

Moonbeams flicker, secrets shared,
Each glimmer shows how much we cared.
Within the stillness, stories unfold,
In twilight's arms, we're forever bold.

A Radiant Revelation

Dawn breaks with golden rays,
Chasing shadows of darkened days.
Whispers of hope fill the air,
A new beginning, bright and fair.

Each petal blooms in splendid cheer,
Beauty emerges, crystal-clear.
Life awakens from slumber's hold,
As dreams ignite, their stories told.

The sun ascends, a fiery crown,
Casting light on every town.
With every heartbeat, joy ignites,
In a world blessed by morning's sights.

Voices rise in sweet refrain,
A symphony of joy, no pain.
Together we stand, united and free,
In the glow of what's meant to be.

Lightfall of the Spirit

In the stillness, a soft glow,
Whispers of wisdom, deep and slow.
Dreams take flight on feathered wings,
In lightfall's embrace, the spirit sings.

Glimmers shine 'neath a silver veil,
Carrying tales the heart can't tell.
Across the distance, journeys rise,
In light's embrace, the spirit flies.

Each moment sparkles, treasures rare,
A dance of light, a sacred prayer.
In this magic, truth unfolds,
The light within us never grows old.

And in the twilight of our days,
We find the path in myriad ways.
Through lightfall's grace, our spirits blend,
In the circle of life, we transcend.

Shadows Embracing Dawn

In whispers of night, shadows play,
They dance with secrets, drift away.
As dawn's light breaks, they fade from view,
Embracing hope in morning's hue.

A canvas painted with soft glow,
Where dreams awaken, gently flow.
Shadows retreat, the world ignites,
In golden rays, the heart takes flight.

The quiet hush before the blaze,
An orchestra of light displays.
Nature stirs as colors blend,
Night's gentle hold begins to end.

Yet in the corners, dark still clings,
A reminder of the night's soft sings.
But dawn brings warmth, a tender spark,
Illuminating paths from dark.

Hand in hand with light's advance,
Shadows bow in morning's dance.
Together they weave, day and night,
In every dawn, a new delight.

Within the Core

Deep in the heart, a fire glows,
Within the core, the spirit flows.
Embers crackle, soft and bright,
A dance of warmth in the silence of night.

Beneath the layers where dreams reside,
A sacred space where thoughts collide.
Fears dissolve in the vibrant haze,
Awakening the soul in a gentle blaze.

Cada heartbeat fuels the flame,
Each pulse reminds us we're not the same.
Whispers echo, secrets to share,
In this quiet place, free from despair.

Cradled softly in the embrace,
Of knowledge deep, our hidden place.
Revelations twine, like roots of a tree,
Nurturing the growth of you and me.

So delve into the depths, explore,
Find strength and wisdom at the core.
From darkness arises the softest light,
Guiding us through the deep of night.

Illumined Pathways

Beneath the stars, the pathway glows,
A gentle light where the river flows.
Guiding footsteps through shadowed trails,
Connecting hearts where love prevails.

Each step unfolds a tale of grace,
In the quiet night, we find our place.
Illuminated by hope's embrace,
A journey shared, at our own pace.

The whispers of the wind invite,
As lanterns dance in the soft twilight.
Each flickering flame, a moment held,
A promise made, a dream compelled.

With every breath, the night unfolds,
Secrets keeper, softly told.
Pathways lit by starlit dreams,
Leading us through the gentle streams.

So walk with me, through twilight's call,
Together we rise, together we fall.
In the luminescence, hearts will stay,
Illumined pathways, come what may.

Flares of Serenity

In the stillness, moments freeze,
Flares of light dance with the breeze.
A gentle flicker, a calming glow,
In this silence, our souls will grow.

Beneath the stars, we find our peace,
With every heartbeat, tensions cease.
An oasis found, where spirits soar,
Flares of serenity, forevermore.

Each sigh whispered, a soothing balm,
In the chaos, find the calm.
Nature's notes in harmony play,
Guiding us through the night and day.

In twilight's gaze, we softly sway,
Lost in thoughts that drift away.
The world's demands may come and go,
But here with you, my heart will know.

So let the flares ignite the night,
A beacon of love, a guiding light.
In moments shared, we've come to see,
Flares of serenity set us free.

Threads of Lucidity

In the quiet of the night,
Thoughts weave through the air,
A tapestry of dreams,
Stitched with silent care.

Visions dance like shadows,
Glowing in the dark,
Wisps of fleeting clarity,
Embers ignite a spark.

Each moment holds a secret,
A whisper soft and pure,
In the depths of lucidity,
We find what we endure.

The mind, a fragile river,
Flows gently through the soul,
Connecting every heartbeat,
Making pieces whole.

A glimpse beyond the chaos,
Where silence starts to sing,
Threads of lucid moments,
In the tapestry we bring.

The Light That Guides

In the depths of the storm,
A beacon starts to rise,
A flicker of commitment,
Beneath the darkened skies.

With every step we're taken,
It shines a path so clear,
Through shadows wrapped in whispers,
Its warmth will hold us near.

Though trials may surround us,
And doubts begin to creep,
The light that guides our journey,
Shall never fade nor sleep.

As embers glow in twilight,
Together we shall stand,
With courage as our armor,
And hope held in our hand.

For every heart that's wandering,
In search of solace true,
The light that guides forever,
Will always shine for you.

Elysian Flames

In the grove of golden whispers,
Elysian flames ignite,
They dance upon the petals,
In the soft embrace of night.

Their warmth a gentle promise,
Of passion, bright and pure,
In every flicker, history,
Of souls that once endured.

The fire sings of freedom,
In colors bold and bright,
With every rise and fall,
A celebration of the light.

In shadows, love ignites,
Drawing hearts to join the dance,
Glowing softly in the twilight,
At the mercy of romance.

Elysian flames forever,
In harmony they sway,
A legacy of beauty,
Guiding us along the way.

Celestial Whispers

In the hush of the cosmos,
Stars breathe a silent tune,
Celestial whispers swirling,
Beneath the watchful moon.

Galaxies hold their secrets,
In patterns yet unseen,
Echoes of ancient stories,
In the celestial sheen.

We float through endless stardust,
Each moment forged in light,
In the arms of the universe,
We find our place so right.

Dreamers dream of wonders,
As planets spin and twirl,
In the dance of creation,
We spin this fleeting pearl.

Celestial whispers calling,
In the heart of night so deep,
We hear the song of starlight,
As the universe takes sleep.

The Heart's Glow

In silence, love begins to bloom,
A gentle light dispels the gloom.
With every whisper, soft and low,
The warmth within begins to grow.

Emotions dance, a tender spark,
Illuminating shadows dark.
Through trials faced, we find our way,
The heart's glow brightens every day.

A bond unbroken, strong and true,
In the depths, where feelings stew.
With every beat, a song takes flight,
Guiding us through the darkest night.

Together we create a space,
Where love's embrace is filled with grace.
With open hearts, we face the show,
In every heartbeat, the heart's glow.

Dawn of Awareness

A new day breaks with gentle light,
Awakening dreams that take their flight.
The sun peeks in, a warm embrace,
Illuminates our hidden space.

In stillness, thoughts begin to rise,
Unlocking truths behind the skies.
With every moment, we unfold,
The stories waiting to be told.

Eyes opened wide, we see anew,
The beauty in the world so true.
Each breath, a chance to understand,
The gentle whispers, life's demand.

Embracing change, we learn to grow,
In the dawn of awareness, knowledge flows.
With hearts aligned, we start to see,
The wondrous path of being free.

Glistening Paths

Through the woods, where shadows play,
Glistening paths lead us away.
With every step, the earth does sing,
A melody of life in spring.

Amidst the leaves, the sun cascades,
Dancing warm through golden glades.
Nature's touch, a soft embrace,
Guiding us through time and space.

Footprints fade, yet memories stay,
Whispers of the trails we sway.
In twilight's glow, we find our peace,
Within these paths, our souls release.

The journey's rich, with tales to share,
In every corner, love and care.
As stars emerge, we find our way,
On glistening paths, we choose to stay.

Embers of Truth

In the night, the fire burns bright,
Embers glow, shedding soft light.
Whispers of fate carry through,
Unveiling secrets, old and new.

Each flicker tells a story grand,
A journey shaped by fate's own hand.
Through ashes, we uncover the raw,
The ember's spark, the eternal law.

In shadows cast, we search for flame,
Seeking answers, none the same.
Truth may hide, but never leaves,
In every heart, the spirit grieves.

As night unfolds, we learn to see,
The wisdom found in mystery.
With courage, we embrace the night,
From embers of truth, we seek our light.

Color in the Gloom

In shadows deep, where silence dwells,
A whisper of hues, a tale it tells.
Crimson dreams on faded walls,
Hope sneaks in as darkness falls.

Flickers bright, a stray spark found,
In every corner where fears surround.
Teal and gold, a hidden scheme,
Painting light upon a dream.

Beneath the weight of midnight skies,
A canvas draped where color lies.
Emerald glints embrace the gray,
Shifting tides, they find their way.

Together they dance, a fleeting show,
In the grip of night, they twirl and flow.
Each stroke a fight, each shade a sigh,
In the gloom where colors lie.

So let the shadows bear their hue,
In the quiet thrum, they pulse anew.
A symphony formed through the veils of night,
Revealing the beauty, igniting the light.

The Essence of Glow

Softly it swells like morning air,
A flicker of warmth, a gentle flare.
In whispered tones, the daylight sings,
Embracing all with tender wings.

Each petal shines, a beacon bright,
Reflecting dreams in golden light.
Through dew-kissed leaves, attention flows,
In every heart, the essence grows.

It dances on waves of languid streams,
In ripples, it stirs lost hopes and dreams.
From shadows cast by twilight's grace,
A radiant pulse takes its place.

As night unfurls its velvet cloak,
Within the dark, a spark awoke.
It lingers on stars, a whispered call,
In the essence of glow, we find it all.

So chase the signs, let your spirit rise,
With every heart, the glow replies.
A luminous thread through space and time,
In the essence of glow, we find our rhyme.

Arcane Beams

Caught in the web of ancient lore,
Arcane beams drift from yonder shore.
Whispers of magic in twilight's embrace,
Emerge with grace, time's tender trace.

Between the folds of celestial light,
Mysteries brew in the heart of night.
Silvered shadows whisper and twine,
Within their dance, the secrets align.

Glimmers of knowledge, secrets unfold,
In every flicker, a story is told.
Fractals of fate twist and bend,
With arcane beams that never end.

The universe hums in silent tongues,
Echoes of ancients, their songs still sung.
Through timeless paths, the whispers guide,
In every heart, the magic resides.

So heed the beams where dreams converge,
In shadows they wait, a vibrant urge.
For within the night, the world believes,
In every soul, arcane beams weave.

Illuminated Solitude

In quiet corners, shadows play,
Illuminated thoughts drift away.
A single light, a faithful friend,
In solitude, we slowly mend.

The flicker of candles, soft and low,
In whispered moments, connections grow.
Silence speaks, a tender sound,
In drifting dreams, solace is found.

Gentle reflections on polished glass,
A world unseen through moments that pass.
In stillness, the heart learns to soar,
The symphony of calm at its core.

Lives brushed gently by the night,
Where shadows bloom in soft moonlight.
Each heartbeat echoes, a lullaby,
In illuminated solitude, we fly.

Hand in hand with the stars above,
We find our way, guided by love.
In the embrace of night's sweet care,
Illuminated solitude, beyond compare.

The Quiet Flame

In the silence, a whisper glows,
A flicker of warmth in shadowed corners,
Embers dance in the hush of night,
A heart beats soft, igniting hope.

Gentle light against the dark,
A beacon found in the tranquil sea,
Guiding souls through fear's embrace,
Where dreams ignite and spirits rise.

The quiet flame, steadfast and true,
Feeds the courage tucked away,
A spark unseen, yet felt within,
In stillness, passions come alive.

Embrace the warmth it brings to life,
A tender glow, a soothing balm,
In chaos, it finds its place,
Radiance born from gentle strife.

So let it dance, this quiet flame,
Through every doubt and every tear,
For even when the night grows long,
Its light will guide us ever near.

Illuminating Shadows

In the stillness, shadows breathe,
Their tales entwined in moonlit hue,
Whispers echo in the night,
Illuminating paths we wander.

Every corner holds a story,
A dance of light and dark combined,
As visions shift and worlds collide,
In every shadow, dreams reside.

The shimmer glows, revealing truths,
Hidden beneath the surface still,
With every flicker of the light,
New horizons start to fill.

Illuminating fears and hope,
In the tapestry of life's great play,
We find our place amidst the dark,
And wear our shadows proudly, brave.

So let the light grow fierce and bold,
For every shadow seeks the sun,
Together, they define the night,
In unity, our journey's won.

Resurgence of Luminosity

From the depths, a radiant call,
Where darkness once held firm and fast,
Hope emerges from quietude,
A resurgence, a light reborn.

Healing whispers rise like mist,
In the dawn of a brand-new day,
Each moment, a flicker of grace,
Resilient hearts, we find our way.

Illuminating paths anew,
As shadows wane and fears recede,
The future brightens with our dreams,
A tapestry of light we weave.

In every heartbeat, luminescent,
Each breath a promise, bold and true,
We stand together, hand in hand,
In this journey, we will break through.

So rise, oh light, in all your form,
Embrace the beauty yet unseen,
For in the dark, we've found our song,
A symphony of hope's bright sheen.

Fanning the Inner Fire

A spark within ignites the soul,
A flickering touch, a guiding flame,
In the heart's depths, it finds its home,
Fanning the glow, fueling our claim.

Whispers of strength swirl in the night,
Each breath a promise, fierce and bold,
Through trials faced, the fire grows,
In every story, courage told.

Gather the flames, let them unite,
Together, they forge paths unknown,
In the warmth of dreams, we rise,
A tapestry of passion sown.

With hands outstretched, we tend the fire,
A shared spark, a global light,
In the darkest hours, we remember,
Our inner flame can chase the night.

So fan it well, this inner fire,
Nurture each flicker, let it soar,
For in every soul, a blaze awaits,
Illuminating what we stand for.

Shimmering Dreams

In the night, stars alight,
Whispers float on gentle air,
Beneath the moon's silver smile,
Dreams take flight without a care.

With each breath, hope awakens,
Drifting soft on twilight's seam,
Drawing paths through endless skies,
Chasing shadows of the dream.

Laughter dances in the dark,
Flickers bright like fireflies,
Each wish cast, a shooting star,
Painting stories in the skies.

Estranged worlds collide so sweet,
Magic woven in the light,
Touching hearts with endless grace,
Moments fleeting, pure delight.

In the dawn, dreams softly bend,
Fading echoes of the night,
Yet the shimmer lingers on,
In our hearts, forever bright.

Heart's Guiding Flame

In the quiet, embers glow,
A flicker warms the weary soul,
Guided by the tender light,
A beacon through the darkened hole.

When shadows creep and fears arise,
The flame within begins to soar,
Each heartbeat synchronizes,
To the rhythm we adore.

Nurtured flames of love ignite,
Chasing doubt with every spark,
Radiating sweet embrace,
Lighting pathways in the dark.

Through storms and trials, it remains,
A steadfast guide through thick and thin,
With every flicker, hope remains,
A promise held deep within.

Let it glow, this flame divine,
An eternal dance of grace,
For in our hearts, it intertwines,
A guiding light, a warm embrace.

Crystalline Vistas

Peaks of glass touch azure skies,
Fragile dreams in sunlight gleam,
Breezes carry whispered tales,
Mountains echo as we dream.

Through valleys deep, rivers glide,
Each drop a gem, each wave a rhyme,
Nature's canvas, art divine,
Crafting beauty, lost in time.

Snowflakes dance on winter's breath,
Shimmering like fleeting hopes,
Caught in prisms of the mind,
Where time and memory elopes.

Cascades tumble, crystal clear,
A chorus sings of peace anew,
In these vistas, hearts find rest,
A tranquil space where dreams ensue.

With every step, the world unfolds,
Mirrored reflections softly spin,
In crystalline, our spirits soar,
Connected to what lies within.

Radiance Within

In the stillness, a spark ignites,
Shining bright from deep inside,
Kindling warmth in every heart,
A glow that cannot be denied.

With every breath, we find our way,
Through shadows that may cloud the sight,
But in our core, a light remains,
A force of love, a guiding light.

As tides recede and waters rise,
Hope ignites the darkest sea,
Finding strength in what we are,
Radiance, our legacy.

In moments fleeting, bright and rare,
Resilience shines through trials faced,
A treasure held within our grasp,
For in this light, we find our place.

So let it glow, this inner fire,
With every beat, let it expand,
A flame that shapes the path we walk,
Radiance within, forever grand.

Radiance Within

In the heart where dreams reside,
A flicker of hope will abide.
With every pulse, a light ignites,
Guiding us through darkest nights.

Whispers dance in twilight's glow,
Softly leading where love flows.
Embrace the warmth, let it unfold,
A treasure trove of stories told.

Hidden strength within us lies,
Shimmering like starry skies.
Boundless joy in every breath,
Celebrating life, defying death.

Whispered Reflections

In stillness, secrets softly speak,
Mirrored thoughts, the answers seek.
Shadows weave the tales of old,
Gentle echoes, memories bold.

Each moment holds a fleeting grace,
Softly fading, time's embrace.
In whispered dreams, we find our way,
Navigating night into day.

Tides of change, they ebb and flow,
Guiding hearts where love shall grow.
In the silence, we connect,
Treasured truths we can't neglect.

Luminescence of the Soul

Deep within, a fire glows,
A radiant light that overflows.
In quiet moments, let it shine,
Illuminating every line.

With every beat, the spirit sings,
An anthem of what wisdom brings.
Through shadows, it will always guide,
An endless river, a flowing tide.

In unity, we find our grace,
A boundless world, a sacred space.
Embrace the journey, feel the spark,
In every heart, a glowing mark.

Glimmers of Solitude

In silence, solitude unveils,
The quiet truth where beauty hails.
Stars above, a guiding light,
In stillness, dreams take flight.

Moments linger, soft and rare,
Whispers echo through the air.
Finding strength in paths we roam,
The heart discovers, finds its home.

From shadowed corners, light will sprout,
A gentle glow that chases doubt.
Embrace the peace that solitude brings,
In the quiet, our spirit sings.

Flickers in the Twilight

Day's last whispers slowly fade,
Colors blend, a soft cascade.
Stars awake, a gentle sigh,
Night wraps all in velvet sky.

Moonlight dances on the stream,
Casting shadows, like a dream.
Crickets sing their evening tune,
As fireflies twirl 'neath the moon.

Voices echo through the trees,
Carried softly by the breeze.
Time stands still, a fleeting glance,
In this hushed, celestial dance.

Whispers of the day now gone,
Echo softly, heart's sweet song.
Twilight holds its breath in pain,
Awaiting dawn's first light again.

In this hour, life feels so right,
Shadows play in tender light.
Moments pass, yet linger near,
Flickers of hope, bright and clear.

Soul's Shining Thread

In the tapestry of fate,
Threads of silver, gold innate.
We weave dreams with every breath,
A connection born from depth.

Through the noise, a song we find,
Melodies that bind and unwind.
Woven hearts in soft embrace,
Hold the universe's grace.

Every joy, a stitch divine,
Every sorrow, a perfect line.
Intertwined, we dance and sway,
As night turns gently into day.

Colors shift with every turn,
Lessons learned, the fire burns.
In the fabric of the night,
Our souls shine, a beacon bright.

Together, we tell this tale,
In the light, we will prevail.
Soul's thread running through us all,
In this dance, we'll never fall.

Enigmas of Illumination

In shadows deep, the truth does hide,
Secrets murmur, mystery wide.
Stars above, their stories spin,
In twilight's glow, the dreams begin.

Questions whispered in the dark,
Flickering with each small spark.
Light reveals what once was veiled,
Through the maze, our hearts are scaled.

Reflections catch the morning dew,
Mirroring paths we journey through.
Enigmas dance in radiant dreams,
Life's puzzles stitched in golden seams.

In lost moments, wisdom grows,
Each bright thought, a petal flows.
Illuminate the road ahead,
Follow where the light is spread.

In silence, shadows start to weave,
All the truths that we perceive.
Boundless visions, fate and chance,
In illumination's trance.

Fragments of Brilliance

Scattered stars across the night,
Each a spark, a flickered light.
Fragments gleam in darkened skies,
Whispers of the cosmos rise.

In the quiet, hope ignites,
Guiding souls with whispered sights.
Every moment's a small gem,
In the heart, they softly stem.

Time unfolds its fragile wings,
As the universe softly sings.
Magic blooms in shadows cast,
Echoes of the future past.

Painted skies, a canvas wide,
Revealing secrets we confide.
Brilliance caught in eyes so bright,
Fragments shimmer with pure light.

In the echoes of the day,
Promise lingers, here to stay.
Life's mosaic, bold and grand,
Fragments forming, hand in hand.

A Beacon in the Fog

In the stillness of the night,
A light begins to glow,
Shining through the heavy mist,
Leading hearts to where to go.

Whispers dance upon the breeze,
Softly guiding lost souls near,
Every glimmer, every gleam,
Chasing away all the fear.

Steady flame against the dark,
A promise of the dawn,
With each flicker, hope ignites,
As shadows begin to yawn.

Against the waves, the beacon stands,
Firm in nature's wild song,
Drawing in those weary hearts,
Reminding them they belong.

Through the fog, its warmth extends,
A guide on life's vast sea,
For in the heart of darkness,
There's always a light to see.

The Glow of Stillness

In the quiet of the dusk,
Where shadows start to play,
A gentle glow begins to rise,
As night embraces day.

Whispers of the closing sun,
Offer peace to weary minds,
A moment's pause in life's great rush,
Where beauty often hides.

Stars awaken one by one,
Glinting in the twilight deep,
Each a wish, a dream, a hope,
In silence, secrets keep.

Through the veil of softest night,
The world stands calm and still,
Heartbeat matched with nature's breath,
In harmony, a thrill.

Embrace the glow of quietude,
Let it wrap you tight,
For in the pause of every day,
Resides the purest light.

Shimmering Reflections

Upon the lake, the moonlight dances,
Casting dreams of silver sheen,
Waves whisper tales of ancient times,
In waters calm and serene.

Mirrored skies with stars alight,
Painting stories in the dark,
Every ripple sings a song,
Of journeys yet to embark.

Floating leaves like thoughts adrift,
Carried by the gentle tide,
Each a memory, a fleeting glance,
Of moments never denied.

The world beneath reflects our soul,
In its depths, we find our peace,
From shimmering to tranquil calm,
All sorrows find release.

As dawn approaches, colors blend,
Nature's canvas vast and grand,
In reflections, we will see,
The beauty of life's hand.

Veins of Brightness

Through the forests, light cascades,
In beams of vibrant grace,
Each ray a thread of golden hue,
Weaving through nature's embrace.

Branches stretch like open arms,
Welcoming the sun's warm kiss,
Nature's breath, a living pulse,
In every moment, bliss.

Flowers bloom in radiant hues,
Painting earth with vibrant tones,
In the dance of life, we find,
A chorus wonderfully known.

Streams of light in morning glow,
Chasing shadows far away,
With every heartbeat, life unfolds,
In colors bright and gay.

We walk these veins of brightness,
In joy, we learn to soar,
For in this world of vivid life,
There's always room for more.

Whispered Illuminations

In shadows soft, the whispers flow,
A gentle breeze, a tale of woe,
Light dances where the secrets dwell,
In silence speaks, what hearts repel.

Stars twinkle through the velvet night,
Guiding dreams, igniting light,
Each flicker holds a promise true,
In whispered tones, they call to you.

Through the dark, a path is drawn,
Embrace the dawn; let fears be gone,
The whispers swell, a soothing song,
In their embrace, we all belong.

With every breath, a spark ignites,
Illuminations weave the nights,
Listen close, the echoes ring,
In quietude, our spirits sing.

So close your eyes and dream awhile,
Let whispered lights create a smile,
For in the dark, we find our way,
Illuminated by night and day.

Echoes of the Soul

In chambers deep, where shadows creep,
Echoes of the soul softly seep,
Through silent halls, they wind and weave,
Whispers of love, we all believe.

A heartbeat's thrum, a gentle plea,
Resonates through eternity,
In every note, a story told,
The echoes warm as they unfold.

Drifting clouds in twilight's hold,
Guiding dreams of silver and gold,
Through whispered verses, hearts ignite,
In echoes soft, we find our light.

The stars align, a cosmic dance,
In every twirl, a whispered chance,
With each reflection, we arise,
To meet the gaze of endless skies.

So let the echoes gently guide,
Embrace the truth we cannot hide,
In each soft word, the soul will find,
A tapestry of love entwined.

Luminescence of the Heart

In every beat, a glow does bloom,
Chasing shadows, dispelling gloom,
A warmth that flows from deep inside,
Luminescence where dreams abide.

Nights aglow with memories bright,
Guiding souls in the quiet night,
Through every tear, a sparkle shows,
In luminescence, true love grows.

With every laugh, a light ascends,
A bond that deepens, never ends,
In gentle whispers, promises chart,
The journey paved by the heart.

Through valleys low and mountains high,
Luminescence lights the sky,
It shows the way when hope feels lost,
A beacon bright, no matter the cost.

So treasure each glow, each radiant part,
For in the light, we find our heart,
In every moment, our spirits soar,
Luminescence forevermore.

Glimmers of Hope

In the rubble where dreams lay bare,
Glimmers of hope dance in the air,
A flicker shines against the night,
In fragile hands, the future bright.

From darkest depths, resilience breaks,
Each whispered wish a river makes,
Flowing gently, a soothing balm,
In glimmers found, the spirit's calm.

Through trials faced and battles fought,
A shimmering thread in every thought,
In every heart, a spark ignites,
Guiding souls through lost starry nights.

With open hearts, we rise anew,
Embracing faith, as we pursue,
Each glimmer shines a path so clear,
A guiding light to draw us near.

So cherish hope, let it unfold,
In every glimmer, stories told,
For in its glow, we find the key,
To brighter days and harmony.

Secrets of the Heart

In whispers soft, the heart confides,
Hidden dreams that time abides.
Shadows dance, a silent song,
In the depths, where secrets throng.

Hope unfurls like morning light,
Binding wounds, banishing night.
Every truth an ember's glow,
In the silence, love will flow.

Wounds and scars, they weave a tale,
Of tender hearts that never pale.
With each beat, they intertwine,
In the tapestry, love will shine.

Veils of doubt, they slowly fade,
As courage blooms, unafraid.
Trust the whispers, feel the spark,
In life's journey, light the dark.

Guard your heart, a sacred chest,
Where hopes awaken, spirits rest.
In the stillness, joy resides,
Secrets dance where love abides.

Dawn of Self

Awakened dreams beneath the sky,
A gentle breath, a whispered sigh.
In the mirror, truth reflects,
A quiet strength, the self connects.

New horizons, bright and clear,
With every step, I draw near.
The past dissolves, a shadowed realm,
In present light, I find my helm.

Voices of doubt begin to fade,
In the light, my fears invade.
With every dawn, a chance to grow,
In the garden where I sow.

Embrace the journey, wild and free,
In the depths, I find the key.
The heart's compass leads the way,
In the dawn of self, I'll stay.

Each moment blooms, a fleeting grace,
In stillness found, I find my place.
Courage rises, lifting me,
I am strong, and I am free.

Illuminated Pathways

Through tangled woods, the light appears,
An ancient trail, where wisdom steers.
Step by step, the darkness wanes,
In glowing paths, the soul regains.

Stars align in night's embrace,
With steady heart, I find my place.
Guided by a radiant chart,
In every curve, a brand new start.

Whispers of fate grace my stride,
In the silence, I confide.
Lost and found in the dance of time,
Each step forward feels sublime.

Gentle winds, a guiding breath,
In every joy, I conquer death.
The light remains, a steadfast guide,
Illuminated paths won't hide.

As dawn approaches in soft hue,
Each step reveals what's bold and true.
With eyes wide open to the day,
I walk the illuminated way.

Essence of Clarity

Through tangled thoughts, I seek the light,
A vibrant truth, profound and bright.
In every moment, clarity grows,
As the essence of being flows.

Clouds disperse, the skies unfold,
In the stillness, stories told.
Voices quiet, fears cast aside,
In the heart's realm, I will reside.

With open arms, I greet the dawn,
In every breath, new dreams are drawn.
Vision sharpened, I embrace,
The essence found in every place.

Moments crafted from pure intent,
In wisdom's light, my spirit's bent.
With clarity as my guiding star,
I find my way, no matter how far.

In whispered truths and gentle grace,
I discover love's warm embrace.
Amid the chaos, peace will thrive,
In the essence of clarity, I arrive.

Resonance of Stillness

In the quiet dawn, all is calm,
Whispers of thoughts, a soothing balm.
Nature breathes deep, in gentle sighs,
Soft echoes dance beneath the skies.

Time stands still, a moment's grace,
Silent shadows in a warm embrace.
The heart listens to the muted sound,
In stillness, a world profound.

Stars twinkle softly, a distant call,
Reflecting dreams that softly fall.
In the hush, the spirit grows,
In stillness, life's essence flows.

A canvas blank, yet full of light,
Colors blend in the quiet night.
Each breath a note in the silent song,
Together we'll find where we belong.

Embrace the peace, let go the fight,
In resonance, we find our sight.
Through stillness, hear the universe sing,
A cosmic dance, a sacred ring.

The Radiant Core

In the heart of night, a spark ignites,
Fires of passion, burning bright.
Inner warmth that guides the way,
Through shadows deep, it calls to play.

A golden glow, a guiding star,
In darkest hours, we travel far.
The pulse of life, a rhythmic beat,
In every heartbeat, love's retreat.

Embers smolder in the quiet air,
Whispers of dreams, a silent prayer.
Sparkling hope where fears once lay,
The radiant core lights up the day.

Unified in the warmth we find,
A tapestry of souls entwined.
Illuminated by a gentle flame,
In every heart, we play the same.

To chase the light, a noble quest,
In the core of us, we find our rest.
Together we rise, together we soar,
In unity, we find the core.

Threads of Brilliance

Woven paths of shimmering light,
Intertwined in the depths of night.
Each thread a story, vibrant and bold,
A tapestry of life to behold.

Colors dance in a graceful spin,
Luminous echoes, where dreams begin.
In every twist, a tale unfurled,
Threads of brilliance, a woven world.

From dusk till dawn, they come alive,
In subtle shimmer, hopes derive.
A network of stars across the sky,
In every thread, a reason why.

The fabric strong, yet soft in touch,
Binding our hearts, it means so much.
From every fiber, we create,
A masterpiece of love, our fate.

So gather close, and weave with care,
In threads of brilliance, we will share.
Together we craft a radiant seam,
In every heart, a shared dream.

Echoes of Vitality

In the rhythm of life, we find our way,
Echoes of laughter brightening the day.
Nature's pulse, a vibrant call,
Reminding us to rise, not fall.

With every heartbeat, a dance unfolds,
Stories of courage, that life beholds.
In whispers of wind, we feel the flow,
Fanning the flames of what we know.

Each breath a gift, in the now we soar,
Connecting with all, forever more.
As echoes ring through the vast expanse,
In every moment, we take our chance.

Embrace the fire, let it ignite,
The passion within, an endless flight.
Together we build, together we grow,
In echoes of vitality, we glow.

So dance to the beat of the drum within,
In the heart of existence, let life begin.
With every echo, a story told,
In the tapestry of life, we are bold.

In the Cavern of Stars

In the cavern deep and wide,
Whispers of the night confide.
Glimmers dance on walls so sheer,
Secrets held, a cosmic sphere.

Echoes chase the fading light,
Dreams take flight in velvet night.
Every twinkle, every glow,
Holds the tales of long ago.

Guided by a silver beam,
Lost in wonder, lost in dream.
Stars align, a dance so vast,
Moments cherished from the past.

In this space, lost thoughts arise,
Mirrored in the night's disguise.
Fleeting hours under sway,
In the cavern, night meets day.

Here in silence, wisdom grows,
Infinite, where time flows slow.
The universe, a soft caress,
In the stars, we find our rest.

A Radiant Pulse

Feel the rhythm, soft and light,
Beats that echo through the night.
Hearts align with every thrum,
Life awakens, senses hum.

In the silence, beauty swells,
Harmony in whispered spells.
Colors flicker, dances swirl,
As emotions start to unfurl.

Every heartbeat, every sigh,
Reflects the way the moments fly.
In this pulse, a world anew,
Captivated, me and you.

Music flows, a river wide,
Carrying dreams upon its tide.
In the rhythm, truth is spun,
With each laugh, the day is won.

As we breathe, interconnected,
Our stories blend, unprotected.
A vibrant beat, we share it all,
In the pulse, we rise, we fall.

Shadows that Sing

In the corners, shadows creep,
Tales of night they softly keep.
Beneath the moon, they weave and sway,
Whispers of dreams that dance and play.

Softly sung, a lullaby,
Secrets, stories, drifting by.
Gentle echoes of the dark,
Bringing forth a kindred spark.

They bind us in the twilight gleam,
Painting visions from a dream.
In their depths, a melody,
Sings of hope and memory.

Every flicker, every shade,
Holds reflections of the afraid.
Yet in shadows, we find light,
Illuminate the longest night.

With each sigh, the silence breaks,
In the stillness, freedom wakes.
Shadows dance, their voices clear,
In the night, we hold them near.

The Mosaic Within

Fragments whisper, pieces shine,
Stories hidden, yours and mine.
In the puzzle, truths unfold,
A tapestry of dreams retold.

Colors blend in vibrant hue,
Each shard holding something new.
Scattered memories, bold and bright,
Crafting beauty from the light.

Every crack, a meaning spun,
In the chaos, we are one.
Linked by threads of joy and pain,
In each tear, in every gain.

Life a canvas, vast and grand,
Shaped by choices, grains of sand.
In this work, we find our place,
A mosaic of the human race.

Through the cracks, we see the sky,
Fragments loom, yet we can fly.
In our hearts, the vision swells,
For every mosaic, a story tells.

Translucent Visions

In shadows dance the fleeting dreams,
Whispers of light behind the seams.
Mirrors reflecting the soul's soft glow,
Carried away where the soft winds blow.

Glimmers of hope in each silent sigh,
Painting the canvas of the sky.
Colors merge in a spectral blend,
Where visions linger and never end.

Through the haze of a morning mist,
Life's gentle touch, a fleeting twist.
Nature's palette, a vivid embrace,
Drawing us near to a sacred space.

Soft echoes call from the depths of thought,
In every moment, a lesson sought.
Translucent visions, like twilight stars,
Guide our journey, no matter how far.

Fireflies of Thought

In the quiet of night, they begin to glow,
Little sparks of wisdom, their magic we know.
Flickering softly, they dance on the breeze,
Bringing bright ideas with gentle ease.

Each flash a reminder, a moment of grace,
Leading us forward, no need to chase.
They light up the dark with their radiant flight,
Instilling in us the courage to fight.

Captured in jars of our memories dear,
These fireflies flicker, both distant and near.
In the garden of thought, they ignite our dreams,
Shining like diamonds, or so it seems.

Let them guide you through the shadows that cling,
Each little light, a promise they bring.
In the realm of the mind, they play and tease,
Fireflies of thought, forever at ease.

The Glow of Existence

Beneath the stars, we find our place,
In every heartbeat, we sense the grace.
Like embers glowing in the night,
Shadows woven with threads of light.

Each moment whispers of life's embrace,
A tapestry rich, a timeless space.
The glow of existence, a sacred hymn,
Resonating softly, within and brim.

In the ebb and flow, we rise and fall,
Echoes of laughter, a shimmering call.
Held in our hearts, the warmth we keep,
In the silence, the depths, we leap.

Embracing the now, we feel the spark,
Guiding us gently through the dark.
In every glance, a reflection shown,
The glow of existence, never alone.

Metaphor of Light

In every shadow, a story hides,
A metaphor of light that abides.
Through dim corridors, it flickers bright,
Illuminating paths with its gentle light.

Wisdom wrapped in rays of the sun,
Guiding our journeys, as we run.
Each glimmer a truth, each spark a guide,
Leading the way with unwavering stride.

In the echo of laughter, in the sighs of pain,
The metaphor of light will always remain.
A solace in darkness, a beacon of hope,
Helping us navigate, learning to cope.

From dawn until dusk, it paints the skies,
Whispering secrets, where beauty lies.
In the heart of the night, it softly unfolds,
A metaphor of light, as life beholds.

Eclipsing Shadows

In twilight's grasp, we linger slow,
Faint whispers dance in dimming glow.
As silhouettes begin to fade,
The night unveils its secret glade.

With stars that wink, the darkness sighs,
A barrier falls from unseen eyes.
Eclipsing fears, we find our way,
To realms where shadows softly play.

The moon, a guide through veils of night,
Illuminates the hidden flight.
Each heartbeat echoes in the dark,
As dreams ignite a gentle spark.

Unfolding truths in muted tones,
The past and future weave their thrones.
In stillness, mysteries entwine,
As shadows bridge the sacred line.

Awake, we stand in twilight's peace,
Where whispers of the cosmos cease.
Eclipsing shadows, spirits soar,
As night reveals forevermore.

A Quiet Gestalt

In silence deep, the thoughts converge,
A tapestry where echoes surge.
Each thread a whisper, a gentle call,
In unity, we rise and fall.

A moment shared beneath the stars,
A bond that heals, despite the scars.
In every breath, the worlds collide,
A quiet gestalt where souls abide.

Like rivers merging, bold and free,
In silent strength, we come to be.
The tapestry unfolds its grace,
In perfect timing, we embrace.

Through tranquil night, our spirits blend,
In every twist, in every bend.
A mosaic bright, our hearts align,
As one we dance, as hand meets sign.

What once was lost, now finds its hue,
In quiet gestures, ever true.
The whispers linger, softly spun,
In unity, we are as one.

The Flare of Existence

In fleeting moments, life ignites,
A flare of joy in endless nights.
We chase the fire, a fleeting blaze,
In shadows cast by fleeting days.

With every heartbeat, colors bloom,
A vivid dance that lights the room.
Through laughter's spark, we find our way,
In fleeting glimpses of the day.

Life bursts forth in radiant arcs,
Creating constellations, sparks.
Each dream a lantern, warm and bright,
That guides us through the darkest night.

Embrace the light, let worries fade,
In every glare, a choice is made.
A flare of existence, bold and clear,
Reminds us always love is near.

With every breath, we rise and fall,
A symphony beyond our call.
In each small flare, the world can see,
The beauty of our unity.

Reflections on a Dewdrop

Upon the leaf, a droplet clings,
Reflecting all that nature brings.
A world within, so clear and bright,
Captured in dawn's soft, tender light.

A mirror small, yet vast in scope,
Holding the dreams of life and hope.
In fragile beauty, secrets lie,
As moments pause and softly sigh.

Each dewdrop sparkles, pure and rare,
Whispers of dawn hang in the air.
The dawn awakens what was lost,
In tiny prisms, we pay the cost.

With every shimmer, stories weave,
Old memories that heart can cleave.
A transient gem, forever free,
In each reflection, we can see.

As sunlight fades and shadows grow,
The dewdrop holds the day's soft glow.
In fleeting moments, life we trace,
Reflections whisper, time and space.

Luminous Secrets

In shadows deep, where whispers dwell,
A dance of light begins to swell,
Secrets twirl on threads of gold,
Each heart's desire gently unfolds.

Moonbeams trace the hidden path,
Through silent woods, igniting wrath,
In every leaf, a story waits,
In every breath, the world creates.

The stars align, a cosmic tune,
Bringing forth the hidden rune,
A tapestry of dreams in flight,
Woven in the fabric of night.

Embrace the glow, the warmth it brings,
Awakened souls to freedom sings,
With every pulse, the truth will shine,
A luminous fate, forever mine.

In stillness found, the shadows bend,
Secrets shared, the light will mend,
Together we'll ignite the flame,
Luminous whispers call my name.

Awakening to Clarity

In morning light, the world is clear,
Dreams dissolve, and doubts disappear,
With open eyes, we learn to see,
The vibrant truth that sets us free.

Gentle winds blow through the trees,
Awakening hearts, like summer breeze,
In clarity, we find our voice,
In every moment, we rejoice.

Ripples dance upon the lake,
Reflections show the path we make,
With each step, a lesson learned,
In the fires of life, we've burned.

The fog of night begins to fade,
A brighter dawn, the fears invade,
With courage strong, we rise anew,
Awakening to the skies so blue.

In every heartbeat, wisdom grows,
Like blooming flowers, the knowledge flows,
Embrace the light, the truth, the grace,
Awakening to clarity, we face.

Starfire in the Void

Amidst the dark, a spark ignites,
A dance of stars through silent nights,
In the vast void, the dreams emerge,
Starfire whispers and visions surge.

Celestial tides pull at our core,
Memories drift from distant shores,
Within the heart lies a cosmic tune,
In every beat, the night becomes noon.

Galaxies pulse with ancient light,
Guiding souls through the veil of night,
In every shadow, a flicker's flame,
In the silence, we call a name.

As starlit paths unfold above,
In the stillness, we find our love,
With each breath, the universe sings,
Starfire dances on ethereal wings.

Through the vastness, we journey on,
With hope alight, till the break of dawn,
In the void, where dreams collide,
Starfire ignites where we abide.

The Heart's Radiant Pulse

In the stillness, a heartbeat plays,
Echoes of love in whispering ways,
With every thrum, the world aligns,
In the rhythm, our spirit shines.

The pulse of life, a tender sound,
Binding us here, in love profound,
Together we move, a sacred dance,
The heart's own song is our romance.

In valleys deep and mountains wide,
The pulse of love becomes our guide,
Through storms and calm, we forge our path,
In laughter's light, we melt the wrath.

Each beat a promise, a soft embrace,
In every challenge, we find our grace,
As tides will turn, we hold the flame,
The heart's radiant pulse, whispering names.

So let us flow, in harmony sway,
United in love, come what may,
In every pulse, our spirits rise,
The heart's true glow, a gift, a prize.

Sparks of Understanding

In shadows deep where questions dwell,
A flicker shines, a story to tell.
With gentle warmth, it lights the way,
To grasp the truths of yesterday.

The whispers of the heart's desire,
Ignite the thoughts and spark the fire.
Each moment shared, an ember drawn,
Connections forged at the break of dawn.

Through trials faced and lessons learned,
The wheel of progress slowly turned.
A bond unspoken, yet so clear,
With every challenge, we persevere.

Together we walk, hand in hand,
In search of wisdom, bold and grand.
From varied paths and stories vast,
A tapestry of truths amassed.

In this shared light, we come to see,
Understanding blooms like a vivid tree.
Each branch a thought, each leaf a chance,
In unity, we find our dance.

Essence of Enlightenment

In quiet hours, the mind does soar,
A tranquil quest on wisdom's shore.
The pulse of life begins to hum,
Awakening the soul's sweet drum.

Each thought a ripple in the stream,
Unearthing truths that brightly gleam.
The essence flows, a rushing tide,
In every heart, it must reside.

Through gentle words and patient ears,
We cast away our doubts and fears.
In shared reflections, wisdom grows,
In seeking light, our spirits glow.

Beyond the dark where shadows creep,
The seeds of knowing softly seep.
With open hearts, we learn to see,
The path to our own clarity.

The dawn of thought, so pure and bright,
Illuminates the endless night.
With every step, we craft our fate,
In essence, love will resonate.

Hidden Brilliance

In every heart, a spark concealed,
A gem of truth, yet unrevealed.
With quiet grace, it waits and grows,
A radiant light beneath the prose.

Searching deep in the silence found,
The brilliance shimmers all around.
In mundane moments, shadows play,
Yet hidden gems keep doubt at bay.

A glance, a smile, a knowing glance,
In simple acts, our spirits dance.
The layers peel as trust unfolds,
Revealing stories yet untold.

Connections spark like stars at night,
Illuminating paths with light.
We find the beauty held within,
In every loss, a chance to win.

Embrace the depths, the quiet schemes,
In hidden brilliance lie our dreams.
With hearts wide open, we shall see,
The treasures that unite you and me.

Flame in the Silence

In hushed repose where shadows blend,
A flickering flame, our hearts defend.
With every breath, the quiet grows,
In stillness, pure devotion flows.

The whispering winds carry our hope,
Guiding us through life's slippery slope.
In solitude, we find our strength,
The flame illuminates the length.

Each heartbeat echoes in the night,
A dance of spirits, soft and bright.
In silent prayers, our souls unite,
As we embrace the endless light.

Through trials faced and shadows cast,
The flame, our anchor, holds steadfast.
Together we rise, unafraid to roam,
In the silence, we find our home.

Let silence speak, let calm prevail,
In every moment, let love set sail.
For in the quiet, truth is found,
A flame in silence, pure and profound.

Gleams from Within

In the quiet night, a spark ignites,
Softly glowing, breaking the dark.
Whispers of hope in gentle sighs,
Guiding us forth with a tender mark.

A flicker of joy in the shadows cast,
Filling the heart with a warm embrace.
Each gleam a promise, a bond to last,
A dance of light in the stillness of space.

Through trials faced and mountains climbed,
These radiant beams shall light the way.
In every heartbeat, love is entwined,
Fueling the fire that will never sway.

Through storms that rage and tempests howl,
The glow remains, a steadfast friend.
It whispers softly, ink to a soul,
In the heart's canvas, colors blend.

Embrace the gleams that reside within,
Let them guide you to the dawn anew.
With each step forward, a chance to begin,
A journey with light, forever true.

Anointed by Radiance

Beneath the heavens, the starlight falls,
Anointing the earth with grace profound.
Each ray a blessing, nature calls,
A dance of brilliance, light unbound.

In every sunrise, a new refrain,
Golden hues warm the cool of night.
With every heartbeat, joy and pain,
Anointed by radiance, hearts take flight.

Branches sway with the gentle breeze,
Whispers of freedom, sweet and clear.
Nature's embrace puts minds at ease,
A sacred bond that conquers fear.

Time flows onward, yet always stays,
In the glow of twilight, dreams unfold.
Hearts illuminated in wondrous ways,
Living stories of love retold.

So let us shine, let our spirits soar,
With every glance, let our hearts ignite.
In the tapestry woven, forevermore,
We find our peace in the sacred light.

Whispers of Luminous Dreams

In the silence of night, dreams softly weave,
Luminous visions that shimmer and sway.
They call to the heart, urging to believe,
In the magic that dances, lighting the way.

Gentle sighs of the moon softly glow,
Casting shadows on paths unexplored.
Each twinkling star a story to show,
Whispers of dreams, forever adored.

With every heartbeat, the cosmos hums,
A symphony rich with a tender grace.
From the depths of the soul, a rhythm drums,
Guiding each step to a havened place.

Awake in the charms of the mystic night,
Find solace within as the universe gleams.
In the silence, we dance, hearts take flight,
In rhythm with whispers of luminous dreams.

So cradle these visions and hold them near,
For in the night's embrace, we learn to trust.
With each breath taken, cast out the fear,
In the glow of dreams, find hope and hush.

Phoenix of the Soul

From ashes gray, the spirit rises,
A phoenix born from moments past.
With wings of fire and brightened skies,
It soars above, free and steadfast.

In trials faced and lessons learned,
Each flame ignites a deeper grace.
The heart, once heavy, now brightly turned,
Embraces life in a wondrous space.

The echoes of struggles fuel the flight,
A tapestry woven with dreams aflame.
In shadows deep, we find our light,
Awakening to a new name.

Transformed by the heat, we learn to rise,
With every fall, rebirth anew.
In the colors of dawn, strength lies,
For phoenix hearts know what is true.

So let the fire blaze, let passion burn,
In every moment, embrace the whole.
From every setback, return and learn,
For within us lies the phoenix soul.

Fireflies at Dusk

In twilight's gentle embrace, they dance,
A soft glow weaving through the air.
Whispers of magic in a fleeting glance,
Nature's lanterns glimmering everywhere.

They flit through shadows, a playful sigh,
Stars born anew in the dimming light.
Moments freeze as they flutter by,
Painting the dusk with a shimmering flight.

Bright sparks alight on the cool, green grass,
Each flicker tells a story, a dream.
In their presence, time seems to pass,
The world transforms into a magic theme.

As night unfolds its tender quilt,
The silence deepens, yet hearts collide.
In their glow, a warmth is built,
Unseen spirits dance, nowhere to hide.

Fireflies twirl in a sweet ballet,
A fleeting reminder of joy's pure call.
In their light, we find a way,
To chase the darkness, to rise, not fall.

Illuminating Silence

In a world brushed quiet by dusk's touch,
Whispers unfold where thoughts abide.
The stillness embraces, a gentle clutch,
Through hidden chambers, shadows glide.

Each breath becomes a sacred song,
Melodies of peace weave in the night.
In silence, we find where we belong,
Illuminated thoughts cast soft light.

A flicker of hope in the calm so deep,
Dreams awaken from slumber's fold.
In the still, our secrets keep,
Timeless tales waiting to be told.

The stars above begin to peer,
Glimmers of wisdom from ages past.
In illuminated silence, we draw near,
Moments of clarity, fleeting yet vast.

Here in the stillness, the heart can speak,
Words unspoken resonate within.
In the quiet, strength we seek,
Illuminating paths where darkness has been.

Soul's Flickering Spark

In the depths where shadows roam,
A flicker ignites, a radiant sign.
The soul awakens, longing for home,
Yearning to bridge the sacred line.

Through trials faced and battles fought,
Each flicker holds a lesson learned.
In every struggle, wisdom caught,
A flame of resilience forever burned.

In the darkness, a beacon shines,
Guiding the heart through tears and pain.
Amidst the chaos, love intertwines,
Transforming loss into hope again.

The journey unfolds, a winding road,
Every step, a chance to ignite.
In every challenge, we carry the load,
Fueling the spark that births the light.

Embrace the flicker, let it soar,
For within the soul, a fire resides.
A flickering spark forevermore,
In the dance of life, our spirit abides.

Veils of Enlightenment

Behind the veil, mysteries hide,
A tapestry woven with golden threads.
Truths emerge where shadows bide,
In the stillness, the seeker treads.

Each layer peeled reveals the light,
In whispers soft, enlightenment calls.
Wisdom blossoms in the quiet night,
Where the heart's voice gently enthralls.

Through the corridors of time we roam,
Veils swirl like mist around the mind.
In every step, we inch towards home,
The essence of self begins to unwind.

As dawn breaks, veils start to part,
Awakening visions once concealed.
In the dance of light, we find our art,
Truths embraced, our souls revealed.

In this sacred space, we come alive,
Endless layers of love and grace.
Through the veils, our spirits thrive,
Enlightenment's glow, an endless embrace.

Candles in the Mist

In the quiet night they gleam,
Flickering softly like a dream.
Guiding those who seek their way,
Through the dark, they gently sway.

Whispers of light in the fog,
Promises hid in the smog.
Each flame tells a secret tale,
Of hearts that wander, souls that sail.

With every breath, the shadows play,
Dancing lightly, gone astray.
Yet they linger, and they stay,
In the mist where dreams delay.

Candles shine by an unseen hand,
Lighting up this spectral land.
Hope ignites within the chill,
With every flicker, fears stand still.

As the dawn begins to rise,
The mist fades, revealing skies.
The candles flicker, then they wane,
Leaving memory's soft refrain.

Chasing Hidden Stars

In the velvet sky so wide,
Whispers of dreams, they collide.
Voyagers armed with hope and fire,
Chasing stars that never tire.

Through the night their wishes soar,
Hoping for a bright encore.
Each twinkle is a secret sign,
Of paths unknown, of fates divine.

They dance above with cosmic grace,
In the heart of the endless space.
Guiding those who dare to seek,
The beauty found in silence sweet.

With every heartbeat, voices call,
To rise above, to never fall.
Hidden stars in realms afar,
We reach out, our guiding star.

In the dark, we find our way,
Chasing dreams that brightly play.
Illuminated by their light,
We journey on through endless night.

Emanation of Hope

In the dawn's gentle embrace,
Hope awakens, finds its place.
With each ray, the shadows flee,
Whispering softly, just to be.

Flowing like a river's song,
Hope reflects where hearts belong.
Each droplet sparkles, clear and bright,
Guiding souls through darkest night.

In the silence, dreams take flight,
Carried forth on wings of light.
A beacon shining through the pain,
Emanation from the rain.

Through the trials, we will rise,
Resilient hearts in endless skies.
With every struggle, love will cope,
In the shadows grows our hope.

So take my hand, we'll walk along,
Together strong, where we belong.
In this dance of life, we'll find,
Emanation ties our mind.

Shadows Embracing Glow

In the twilight where dreams meet,
Shadows dance on nimble feet.
Gentle whispers fill the air,
Embracing light, a tender flare.

Echoes soft in the fading light,
Softly blend with the coming night.
A tapestry of dark and day,
Weaving stories in their play.

Through the dusk, a warmth appears,
Comfort found among our fears.
Shadows wrap their arms around,
In this glow, our peace is found.

The world transforms, a canvas broad,
Where light and dark become our God.
Together, they navigate the flow,
In the depths of shadows' glow.

Hold tight to dreams as they unfold,
In the dark, our hearts are bold.
For in this realm where contrasts blend,
Shadows hug the light, our friend.

Chasing the Dawn

In the hush of early light,
Whispers of dreams take flight,
Colors blend, a soft embrace,
The world awakes, we find our place.

Footsteps echo through the mist,
Each moment a fleeting twist,
Golden rays begin to rise,
Chasing shadows from the skies.

Nature stirs, the birds all sing,
Hope is born, a vibrant thing,
The night retreats, it fades away,
Dawn's sweet promise starts the day.

With open hearts, we greet the morn,
Every challenge, we adorn,
Together strong, we face the light,
Chasing dreams with all our might.

As the sun climbs ever high,
Painting warmth across the sky,
We find joy in every breath,
Chasing dawn, embracing death.

Beacons of Resilience

In the storm's unyielding rage,
Courage stands, a steadfast gauge,
Hearts united, strong and bright,
We are beacons, glow with light.

When shadows fall and spirits wane,
Together, we will bear the pain,
Like sturdy trees, with roots we bind,
In unity, strength we find.

Every scar tells tales of fight,
From the depths, we seek the height,
Through the trials, we will soar,
Beacons shining evermore.

Flickering flames in darkest night,
Hope ignites our blazing light,
With every step, we forge our way,
Resilience blooms, come what may.

When the world feels cold and bare,
We will rise, a fervent prayer,
Hand in hand, we climb life's hill,
Beacons shining, steadfast will.

Beneath the Surface

In still waters, secrets hide,
Whispers echo, dreams abide,
Beneath the waves, the stories rest,
Depths reveal what we know best.

Ripples dance and shadows play,
Time flows softly, drift away,
A world unseen, yet so profound,
In silence, life's truths are found.

Coral reefs and fish that glide,
Life unfolds, a secret ride,
From the murky depths, we rise,
With open hearts and curious eyes.

Nature's pulse beats in the deep,
Where the ancient currents sweep,
A treasure trove of hope and dreams,
Beneath the surface, nothing's as it seems.

Dive within, let currents steer,
Face the depths without any fear,
For in the silence lies our worth,
Beneath the surface, life rebirth.

Light as a Gossamer

A fragile thread, a whispered sigh,
Like morning mist, it floats on high,
Delicate patterns weave through air,
Light as a gossamer, tender and rare.

Embracing dreams with a gentle touch,
Where worries fade, and fears mean much,
We dance in colors, softly spun,
Chasing moments, lost in fun.

In twilight's glow, our spirits soar,
Each heartbeat echoes, yearning for more,
Wings like feathers, we drift and glide,
In this realm, we shall abide.

Cocooned in warmth, we find our grace,
Light as a gossamer, we embrace,
In the tapestry of night's retreat,
We find our strength, we won't accept defeat.

A perfect harmony, soft and bright,
Illuminates the velvet night,
Together we rise, hearts entwined,
Light as a gossamer, love defined.

www.ingramcontent.com/pod-product-compliance
Ingram Content Group UK Ltd.
Pitfield, Milton Keynes, MK11 3LW, UK
UKHW021309280125
4330UKWH00005B/187